Natural Disasters

Earthquakes

by
Allison Lassieur

Consultant:
John R. Reid, Ph.D.
Professor Emeritus of Geology
University of North Dakota

CAPSTONE BOOKS

an imprint of Capstone Press
Mankato, Minnesota

Capstone Books are published by Capstone Press
151 Good Counsel Drive, P.O. Box 669, Mankato, Minnesota 56002
http://www.capstone-press.com

Library of Congress Cataloging-in-Publication Data
Lassieur, Allison.
  Earthquakes/by Allison Lassieur.
  p. cm.—(Natural disasters)
  Includes bibliographical references and index.
  Summary: Describes how and why earthquakes happen, the damage they can
cause, ways they are measured, and some of the most destructive quakes of the past.
  ISBN 0-7368-0586-9
  1. Earthquakes—Juvenile literature. [1. Earthquakes.] I. Title. II. Natural disasters
(Capstone Press)

QE521.3.L39 2001
551.22—dc21   00-020876

Editorial Credits
Connie R. Colwell, editor; Timothy Halldin, cover designer and illustrator;
  Kia Bielke, illustrator; Heidi Schoof and Kimberly Danger, photo researchers

Photo Credits
Archive Photos, 28
Betty Crowell, 34
Bill Brockett/Pictor, 41
Chromosohm/Sohm/Pictor, 8
Clark Dunbar/Pictor, 10
Doug Milner/Pictor, 20
Express Newspapers/Archive Photos, 26
FPG International LLC/Spencer Grant, 44
International Stock/Elliott Smith, cover; Horst Oesterwinter, 15; Tom Carroll, 16,
  36; Warren Faidley, 18
Mary Altier, 32
Reuters/Michael Dalder/Archive Photos, 4; Reuters/Stringer/Archive Photos, 6;
  Reuters/Bob Strong/Archive Photos, 30
Unicorn Stock Photos/Tommy Dodson, 46
Visuals Unlimited/CP George, 22; Albert Copley, 39

1 2 3 4 5 6 06 05 04 03 02 01

Table of Contents

Chapter 1

Earthquakes

At 3 a.m. on August 16, 1999, a loud rumbling disturbed the people of Izmit, Turkey. The ground shook. Objects fell from shelves and cabinets. Tall buildings swayed and collapsed. Bricks and debris fell from the buildings.

The earthquake was one of the most powerful to hit Turkey in more than 10 years. More than 17,000 people died during the earthquake. Many of these people died when their apartment buildings collapsed. The earthquake also destroyed thousands of homes. It even destroyed buildings in Istanbul. This city is more than 65 miles (105 kilometers) from Izmit.

The 1999 earthquake in Izmit, Turkey, killed more than 17,000 people.

The earthquake destroyed many buildings in Izmit.

Some parts of Izmit were destroyed. The buildings were reduced to piles of brick and concrete. Homeless people wandered through the streets. Rescue workers dug through the debris looking for survivors.

Three months later, another large earthquake hit the area. Buildings weakened by the first earthquake collapsed. Hundreds of people died.

Earthquakes

Thousands of small earthquakes occur around the world every day. These earthquakes may rattle windows. They may sound and feel like a huge truck driving down the street. But most earthquakes are so mild that people do not notice them.

Earthquakes the size of the Izmit earthquake are rare. These earthquakes can topple buildings, collapse bridges, destroy roads, and injure or kill people. They can cause millions of dollars in damage.

Chapter 2

Why Earthquakes Happen

Long ago, people did not understand why earthquakes occurred. People around the world created legends to explain these disasters. Today, scientists know that these stories are not true.

Earthquake Legends

In India, some people believed that eight elephants held up Earth. These elephants lowered their heads when they became tired. People believed this motion caused earthquakes.

People in other parts of the world created different stories about earthquakes. Some American Indians believed that Earth was

People around the world created legends to explain why earthquakes occurred.

9

balanced on a turtle's back. Earthquakes occurred when the turtle moved. An African story explained that Earth was balanced on the head of a giant. Earthquakes occurred when the giant sneezed. Many Japanese people believed that a giant catfish named Namazu held Earth. Earth shook when the giant fish flipped.

Earth's Layers

The crust forms the Earth's surface. This rocky material covers the entire Earth. This area includes the area beneath the oceans. The crust is between 5 and 25 miles (8 and 40 kilometers) thick.

The Earth's crust is broken into pieces. The pieces form a pattern like a cracked eggshell. The different pieces of the crust are called plates. The crust includes about 10 large plates and 20 smaller plates.

A layer of hot rock lies beneath the crust. This layer of Earth is called the mantle. The

The crust forms the Earth's surface. ⟵

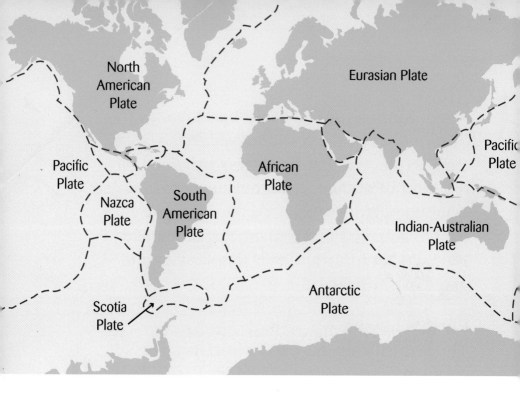

crust's plates extend down to the upper part of the mantle.

Plate Movement

Heat from the lower mantle causes the plates to move. The plates move slowly over the lower mantle. Plates move only about as fast as fingernails grow.

Earthquakes can occur when two plates move apart. They also can occur when plates bump or scrape against each other.

Earthquakes usually occur near plate edges. Plate movement causes friction. This force is created when two objects rub against each other. Friction can make plates stick together. It also prevents the plates from moving.

The heat from the lower mantle continues to push or pull the plates. Pressure builds up in the areas where plates are stuck. This pressure eventually breaks apart the plates. This force sends out shock waves that shake the ground. This occurrence is an earthquake.

Where Earthquakes Occur

Three-fourths of the world's earthquakes occur along the Ring of Fire. This area surrounds the Pacific Ocean. The Ring of Fire includes Japan, northern Asia, and the west coasts of South and North America.

Many earthquakes also occur near the Mediterranean Sea. This area includes Southeast Asia and the Middle East.

Plate edges where movement can occur are called faults. Most faults are not visible. Soil covers them.

The San Andreas Fault in California is one of the world's most famous faults. This fault is about 750 miles (1,200 kilometers) long. The two plates that cause the San Andreas Fault are very active. This fault causes many earthquakes to occur in California.

Another large fault lies along the coast of Asia. Many earthquakes occur along this fault near Japan.

Related Storms

The heat from the mantle sometimes becomes so hot that it rises through Earth's crust. Hot, liquid rock called magma bursts forth. This explosion of magma is called a volcanic eruption.

The San Andreas Fault in California is about 750 miles (1,200 kilometers) long.

Earthquakes always accompany volcanic eruptions. The upward movement of the magma causes the crust to move.

Earthquakes can cause destructive forces. The shaking motion can cause loose rocks, soil, or snow to fall from higher places such as mountains. This occurrence is called a landslide. The loose objects often damage land and property as they fall. Landslides even can injure or kill people and animals.

Earthquakes also can cause mudflows. An earthquake's force can cause loose ground to collapse and mix with ground water or rain. This causes mud to form. Mud can flow down hills and cause damage. Mud also can behave like quicksand. Buildings, automobiles, and other objects can sink into the ground.

Earthquakes that occur beneath the ocean can cause tsunamis. Tsunamis often are called tidal waves. The motion of the plates beneath the ocean can cause ocean water to rise and fall. High waves can form. These waves can destroy boats and houses in surrounding areas. Tsunamis also can cause floods. In 1946, a tsunami hit Hawaii. This wave was so strong that it bent parking meters in half.

Earthquakes can create tsunamis that travel around the world and hit shores thousands of miles away. In 1960, an earthquake in Chile, South America, caused a tsunami that hit Hilo, Hawaii, and Japan the next day. The 20-foot (6-meter) waves killed more than 100 people.

Earthquakes can cause mudflows.

Other Effects

The effects of an earthquake can be more deadly than the earthquakes themselves. Earthquakes can damage water lines and dams. This damage then can cause floods. Damaged electricity and gas lines can cause fires.

Small earthquakes called aftershocks often occur after major earthquakes. Weakened buildings and structures that withstood large earthquakes may collapse during aftershocks.

Aftershocks often occur after major earthquakes.

Chapter 3

The Power of an Earthquake

An earthquake is one of the most powerful forces on Earth. Scientists hope to learn more about earthquakes' power. This knowledge may help prevent earthquake damage.

Seismographs

Seismologists are scientists who study earthquakes. Seismologists measure the power of earthquakes with an instrument called a seismometer. This instrument detects underground motion caused by earthquakes.

A seismometer consists of an underground rod, a hanging weight, a piece of paper, and a pen. The underground rod detects vibrations

An earthquake is one of the most powerful forces on Earth.

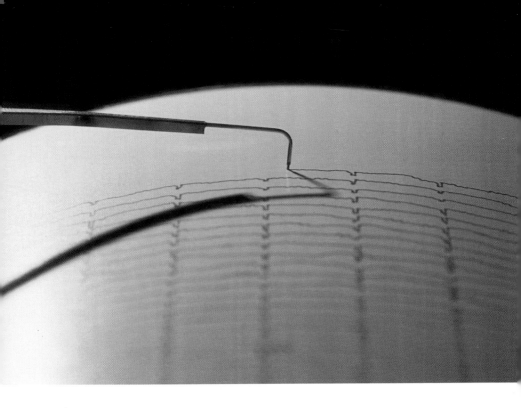

Seismometers record earthquakes' power.

from earthquakes. The rod is attached to the hanging weight. The weight remains stable as the rod moves up and down or back and forth. A pen attached to the weight moves with the rod. This movement causes the pen to draw lines on the paper. These lines form a report called a seismograph.

Seismographs tell seismologists how strong an earthquake is. Strong earthquakes cause the rod to move more noticeably than weak earthquakes. This will cause the pen to draw longer lines on the paper. Short lines on a seismograph indicate a weak earthquake.

The Mercalli and Richter Scales

In 1902, an Italian seismologist named Giuseppe Mercalli developed a scale to measure the power of earthquakes. He called it the Mercalli scale. This scale reflected the amount of damage caused by earthquakes. Low numbers on the Mercalli scale indicated an earthquake that caused little damage. High numbers indicated a more destructive earthquake.

In 1931, two American seismologists improved the Mercalli scale. Today, the scale is called the modified Mercalli scale. It identifies earthquakes in much the same way as the older scale. But the modified Mercalli scale reflects damage to modern types of buildings and structures.

The Richter Scale

Richter Magnitude	Earthquakes Per Year	Amount of Damage
1	700,000 or more	Very minor
2	300,000	Very minor
3	300,000	Minor
4	50,000	Light
5	6,000	Moderate
6	800	Strong
7	120	Major
8	20	Major
8+	1 every 5 to 10 years	Great

In 1935, Charles Richter invented another scale that measured earthquakes' power. The Richter scale measures earthquakes' magnitude. Magnitude is the measurement of the force of an earthquake.

The Richter scale rates an earthquake from 1 and up. A measurement of 1 on the Richter scale indicates a small earthquake. These earthquakes are the most common. High numbers on the Richter scale indicate large earthquakes. Some earthquakes register more than 8 on the Richter scale. These earthquakes are rare.

Chapter 4

Famous Earthquakes

Earthquakes can cause a great deal of damage. They can destroy cities and kill or injure millions of people.

Even weak earthquakes can cause destruction. Cities may have poorly constructed buildings or high populations. Weak earthquakes can cause great damage in these types of cities.

Southern Chile, 1960

On May 22, 1960, an 8.3 magnitude earthquake struck southern Chile in South America. The earthquake destroyed small villages and damaged buildings in large cities.

In 1960, an 8.3 magnitude earthquake struck Chile.

Aftershocks continued to hit the area during the next few days. These aftershocks caused huge landslides that buried entire villages. Volcanoes in the area erupted. More than 10,000 people were killed or missing. More than 3,000 people were injured. Two million people were left homeless. The earthquake created a huge tsunami that hit Hawaii, Japan, and the Philippines. The tsunami killed 170 people.

Anchorage, Alaska, 1964

On March 27, 1964, the ground in Anchorage, Alaska, began to shake. Shock waves continued for 5 minutes. The earthquake destroyed most of the buildings in the downtown area. Cracks more than 6 feet (1.8 meters) wide opened up in the roads. In some places, the ground split and sections of earth dropped dozens of feet or meters. More than 30 blocks of the city were completely destroyed. Landslides covered other areas.

In 1964, an earthquake struck Anchorage, Alaska.

In 1985, an 8.1 magnitude earthquake struck Mexico City, Mexico.

This earthquake is considered the most powerful to ever hit the United States. Its magnitude was 9.2. But this earthquake caused few deaths compared to other powerful earthquakes. Alaska does not have a large population. It also has few large cities. About 100 people died during this powerful earthquake.

Mexico City, 1985

On September 19, 1985, an 8.1 magnitude earthquake shook Mexico City, Mexico. This earthquake caused great damage to the downtown area. More than 10,000 people died and 250,000 lost their homes. More than 800 buildings were destroyed.

Few of Mexico City's buildings were constructed to withstand earthquakes. Buildings more than six stories high collapsed. Some swayed more than 3 feet (1 meter) before they collapsed. In some cases, two swaying buildings smashed into each other and then collapsed.

Chapter 5

Surviving an Earthquake

Some scientists try to predict earthquakes. These predictions may prevent people from being injured or killed by further earthquakes. They also may prevent millions of dollars in damage.

Earthquake Predictions

Today, people cannot accurately predict earthquakes. But scientists have some methods they use to attempt to predict earthquakes. The most common method is the seismic gap method. People who support this method believe that pressure builds up along a fault

Today, people cannot accurately predict earthquakes. ◁

33

the pressure becomes too great. The seismic gap method indicates that earthquakes are more likely to occur in areas where one last occurred long ago.

Some seismologists believe that the next large U.S. earthquake will occur in California. A great deal of pressure has built up along parts of the San Andreas Fault. But there is no way to tell if or when this earthquake will occur.

In China, the government tells people to watch for clues in nature that might predict an earthquake. Animals may begin to act strangely. Well water may turn muddy or appear to boil. Small earthquakes may strike before a large one hits. In 1975, the Chinese government used these clues to accurately predict a strong earthquake. But these clues failed to predict a later earthquake.

Earthquake Preparations
Today, most people believe that it is better to prepare for an earthquake than try to predict it.

Scientists study earthquakes in order to learn to predict them.

Strong, stable buildings may withstand earthquakes. Following safety measures helps people survive earthquakes.

The safest place to be during earthquakes is on the ground away from buildings and trees. People should avoid tall buildings, power lines, and overpasses. People also should not stand beneath statues or other structures. These structures may collapse. People should stay away from windows and mirrors. Earthquakes can break or shatter glass.

People also should practice earthquake drills. Earthquake drills are similar to fire drills. These drills help people know what to do if they are trapped inside buildings during earthquakes. People should know the safest places to take cover. Building owners should have this information readily available. For example, people may huddle beneath heavy pieces of furniture for shelter.

People who live in areas where earthquakes often occur should make special preparations. They should choose a safe place to meet their

People should avoid overpasses during earthquakes.

family members when earthquakes occur.
This place may be a nearby open area. Meeting
places can help people keep track of family
members during earthquakes.

People also should ask a friend or relative
from a distant city to be a contact person. All
members of the family should memorize this
person's phone number. Family members who
are separated from the family during an
earthquake can call this person. This person
can give the rest of the family information
and pass along messages.

Strong Buildings

Collapsed buildings injure and kill many
people during earthquakes. City planners try to
design offices, bridges, and other buildings
that can withstand earthquakes. Some of these
buildings have strong braces inside their walls.
Others have special pads and rollers that allow
the buildings to move as the ground shakes.
Some buildings have wide bases and narrow

City planners try to build offices, bridges, and other
buildings to withstand earthquakes.

38

tops. The wide bases make the buildings stable during earthquakes.

A team of scientists at the State University in Buffalo, New York, is designing a new type of building. These scientists hope that these buildings will be able to withstand earthquakes. The scientists have invented a system of special supports that are controlled by computers. These buildings will be able to detect motion during earthquakes. The computers will instruct the supports to push or pull against the walls if the building sways.

People cannot prevent earthquakes. Even the strongest buildings may be damaged or destroyed by an earthquake. But proper preparation measures can help people survive these disasters.

Proper preparation measures can help people live through earthquakes.

Words To Know

collapse (kuh-LAPS)—to fall down suddenly; buildings often collapse during earthquakes.

crust (KRUHST)—the outer layer of Earth's surface

debris (duh-BREE)—broken pieces of buildings and other structures

fault (FAWLT)—a crack in Earth's crust where two plates meet

friction (FRIK-shuhn)—the force that slows down Earth's plates when their edges rub together

magnitude (MAG-nuh-tood)—the size of an earthquake

mantle (MAN-tuhl)—the part of Earth between the crust and the core

seismometer (SIZE-mom-uh-tur)—an instrument used to measure the power of earthquakes

tsunami (tsoo-NAH-mee)—a destructive wave caused by an underwater earthquake

To Learn More

Arnold, Nick. *Volcano, Earthquake, and Hurricane.* The Remarkable World. Austin, Texas: Raintree Steck-Vaughn, 1997.

Morris, Neil. *Earthquakes.* The Wonders of Our World. New York: Crabtree Publishing, 1998.

Ritchie, David. *The Encyclopedia of Earthquakes and Volcanoes.* New York: Facts on File, 1994.

Walker, Sally M. *Earthquakes.* A Carolrhoda Earthwatch Book. Minneapolis: Carolrhoda Books, 1996.

Useful Addresses

**Center for Earthquake Research and
  Information**
University of Memphis
Campus Box 526590
Memphis, TN 38152

Earthquake Engineering Resource Institute
499 14th Street
Suite 320
Oakland, CA 94612-1934

National Geological Survey of Canada
GSC Pacific—Sidney Subdivision
Pacific Geoscience Centre
P.O. Box 6000
Sidney, BC V8L 4B2
Canada

United States Geological Survey
National Earthquake Information Center
P.O. Box 25046
DFC, MS 967
Denver, CO 80225

Internet Sites

ExploreZone.com—Earthquake Science
http://explorezone.com/earth/earthquakes.htm

Nevada Seismological Laboratory
http://www.seismo.unr.edu

Savage Earth Online
http://www.pbs.org/wnet/savageearth

Southern California Earthquake Center
http://www.scec.org

Understanding Earthquakes
http://www.crustal.ucsb.edu/ics/understanding

U.S. Geological Survey
http://www.usgs.gov

Index

19/00

GAYLORD'S